Praise For
"The Newman Adjustment"

The Newman Adjustment is right on
target. It reads quickly, is entertaining, and
offers dozens of insights about what makes
organizations effective. It should be a must read
for technologists, managers, and all
professionals interested in improving
performance and alignment within their
organizations.

Brian Lassiter, President
Performance Excellence Network

Al Strauss' parable brings the needs of a modern organization to life. Workplace adaptability, cooperation and trust can improve both the bottom-line and knowledge worker engagement. This story has important insights for IT, HR, managers and senior leaders alike.

Fred Sheahan,

Learning Environment Engineer,

Prime Digital Academy

Just finished reading this fantastic fable. Al Strauss hit on the two things that count most to me, communication and people. No matter what business you are in, you are in the people business. And the key to people is communication, change and recognition. Hopefully *The Newman Adjustment* will help readers to fully understand and deal with those issues effectively.

Paul Ramig, IT Project Manager (retired)

AgriBank, FCB

This book is fun, informative and packed full of great tips for helping you to better align your business and IS (Information *Services)*. Our hero creates a "win-win" situation for all concerned and he didn't even need to write a single line of code. He understood the business and its needs because he was purposely taught to understand them and made the change by distilling a set of simple practices and used them to transform the company. In this fable, "business" and "IS" alignment becomes a fully integrated "one."

Christian Pedersen, CEO
The Bulldog Companies

The Newman Adjustment is a very interesting read. It spells out some very common sense, but seldom used, approaches to help an organization align its IS team with the various customer groups. Al Strauss completed a hat-trick by highlighting the importance of:

- Building a relationship between the application developers and their customers,
- Proactively training the organizational leaders so they can properly mentor and develop their direct reports,
- Setting expectations early on.

John Prosser, Staff Software Engineer
United Technologies Aerospace Systems

The Newman Adjustment:

A Fable About Bridging The

Gap Between Business And

Software

By

Al Strauss

Al Strauss Consulting
Bloomington, Minnesota

The Newman Adjustment:
A Fable About Bridging The Gap Between Business
And Software
By Al Strauss

Published by
Al Strauss Consulting
11311 Xavier Road
Bloomington, MN 55437

ISBN-10: 1511823429
ISBN-13: 978-1511823425

Published in the United States of America

For my parents

Contents

Foreword: Making The Idea Real

By Glenda H. Eoyang, PhD
Founding Executive Director, Human
Systems Dynamics Institute
(www.hsdinstitute.org)
Author of *Adaptive Action: Leveraging*
Uncertainty in Your Organization **(Stanford**
University Press, 2013)

As information technology, customer expectations, and business environments get more complicated, it seems logical to draw clear lines, allocate responsibilities, and isolate business from technical decisions. There seem to be too many details, too much expertise, and too many perspectives to be absorbed into a single decision-making process. Such an approach may be logical, but as *The Newman Adjustment* clearly demonstrates, to divide is not necessarily to conquer!

Al Strauss has provided us with a wise fable, describing a world where business and technical insights depend on each other, and where the customer's point of view and business needs drive the use of information and information technology. As the parable unfolds, we see the myriad benefits of integrated, team-based decision making:

- The individual's sense of satisfaction and value increase,
- Business processes are improved,
- Technology is applied when and where it is needed most, and
- People come together to share their problems and their solutions.

The ideal world described here may not be your reality yet, but it can be. Whatever your span of control in your organization, you can begin to turn this fiction into fact for you, your teammates, and your organization. By taking to heart the concepts and skills described here, you can see how information and business can unite and conquer!

Preface

The book you are holding in your hands is about making your computer department more of a part of the business. In today's modern world, your company will find it difficult, if not impossible, surviving without software and computers so given its considerable investment, why not maximize its strategic alignment to the business?

Many internal computer departments, whether they are called IT, IS, MIS or any other name, are not as strategically helpful to their organizations as they have the potential to be. This isn't due to indifference or incompetence. It is caused by being misaligned with the rest of the organization, by focusing more on technology than on business needs. Both the internal computer department *and* its internal customers share the responsibility for this situation.

The result of such misalignment? According to the Gallup Business Journal, "A study published in the *Harvard Business Review*, which analyzed 1,471 IT projects, found that the average overrun was 27%, but one in six projects had a cost overrun of 200% on average and a schedule overrun of almost 70%...One estimate of IT failure rates is between 5% and 15%, which represents a loss of $50 billion to $150 billion per year in the United States. Another study estimated that IT project failures cost the European Union €142 billion in 2004."[1]

Putting aside one's political views, look at the rollout for the Affordable Care Act's website in October, 2013. It was universally panned for its performance problems quickly

---

[1] http://businessjournal.gallup.com/content/152429/Cost-Bad-Project-Management.aspx

followed by the blame game. There was plenty of finger-pointing going around; everyone involved seemed to blame everyone other than themselves. Without having direct knowledge of how the website was built, it is a logical guess to say that everyone involved has to share some of the blame. And while software implementations rarely have the national media's scrutiny, these technology failures happen all the time in the business world.

There is also a human cost: frustration, unnecessary overtime, turnover, negative impact on work/life balance, etc.

In the pages that follow, you will be exposed to many ideas and concepts to help combat such waste in your organization by aligning IS with the rest of your company. They may save your company tens of thousands, hundreds of thousands or even millions of dollars over time. They may even make you something of a hero in your organization.

A New Beginning

This fable, like all good fables, will start at the beginning. In fact, this fable will start before the beginning, because John Newman's alarm clock hadn't gone off yet. But he was already awake.

Today is the day John is starting his new job, one of the many changes he and his family had been going through. As he lay in bed, he thought back in the events of his life that brought him to where he is today.

Life was both old and new for John. He and his family had just moved back to his old hometown, Typical Town, the city in which he had grown up, and where he had met and married his high school sweetheart, Marilyn.

After graduating with a degree in computer science from Prestigious University, he and Marilyn moved to Humongous City

1

because that is what they thought young couples with their whole futures ahead of them were supposed to do in order to become successful.

After being recruited by several companies, John had taken a job as a software developer with Humongous Samples (HS), the leading manufacturer of samples. (Whenever a sales representative had to demonstrate a product for a potential customer, a high quality sample was always needed.) Now, several years later, with twin sons to raise, John had taken a new job with one of HS' competitors, TypTown Samples, in order to move back to Typical Town.

When he had called his parents back in Typical Town to tell them about his new job, his father, Ramsey, just chuckled. Ramsey had once worked for TypTown Samples and had retired from the firm with a full pension three years earlier. Now he spent as much time as possible fishing.

John knew it hadn't bothered his father that he had worked for TypTown Samples' competitor for years, because he remembered the many times his father would come home from a tough day on the line, in a bad mood and grousing about what a ridiculous company he worked for.

Ramsey had been a good provider for his family even though he had hated his job. TypTown Samples was Typical Town's largest employer and, although it was not a major player in the sample industry, it was a steady company to work for. Plus, Typical Town was a nice place to raise kids. John knew that his father could have done other things in his life, but he had chosen to live in Typical Town for John's sake.

And now, John thought, he was doing the same things for his sons. The boys, Tony and Kirby, were now old enough to start school. John and Marilyn didn't want their boys to go to school in Humongous City. They remembered how life was in Typical Town and thought it was best for the boys to grow up in that environment.

So John, by now an application developer, had reluctantly resigned from his position at HS to accept a similar position at TypTown Samples. TypTown was more than happy to get a top performer from its primary competitor.

As he lay awake thinking about everything, that reluctance was rapidly turning into certainty that he was making a dreadful mistake. "Like father, like son," he thought, sighing. Then he thought of his grown-up sons someday also working for TypTown Samples. "I'll raise my boys to be smarter than my old man taught me to be," he told himself.

And at that thought, the LCD on John's alarm clock changed from 6:29 to 6:30 and the clock dutifully issued a loud, annoying buzz.

Marilyn grumbled something as she reached over to shut off the alarm clock. John sighed again and got out of bed to prepare for the big day.

John had an unusually light breakfast, for he was too nervous to eat much. Instead, he checked in on the boys, who were still sleeping. John was proud of the sacrifice he was making for his boys. "I'll bet there aren't a lot of dads out there that are willing to throw away their careers for the sake of their kids," he thought, mentally picturing himself with a Father of the Year medallion around his neck.

His wife, reading his mind, kissed him good-bye on his way out the door and said, "You're a terrific father, John. Have a great first day."

John turned back to show the big smile Marilyn had put on his face.

As John walked to the car to begin the short commute to TypTown Samples, he heard his name being called. He looked up to see his next-door neighbor, Wes Turner. John, Marilyn, Wes and Wes' wife Jayne had all grown up together, and the Newmans were happy to be reunited with their old friends and felt fortunate when they were able to buy the house next door.

In addition to being old friends, it turns out that John and Wes also shared the same occupation. Wes was an application developer working for Crusedome Systems, the town's second largest employer. Wes, an outgoing personality if there ever was one, came over to make sure his buddy was fired up for his first day at his new job.

"Hey, John," repeated Wes, "Happy Monday! Are you ready for the big day?"

"Yeah, you bet," said John, hoping to keep his dread a secret.

"TypTown is getting a smart guy. Remember, if you don't like what you see, you should check out CS. We don't have anything open now, but you never know what's going to happen. What's the plan for day one?"

"I imagine today will be all about orientation and filling out forms."

"No one ever accused corporate America of not having enough forms to file."

The small talk continued for a few minutes more, but before long, John was in his car, driving to his new job.

The Heart Of The Company

John turned down the long driveway into the employee parking lot a few minutes later, thinking that he certainly wouldn't miss that long commute he had in Humongous City.

As he parked his car, John took a deep breath, hesitated one last time, then finally got out and walked to the main entrance. Upon entering TypTown Samples' headquarters, he strolled over to the receptionist, took another deep breath, and announced, "I'm John Newman. I'm the new application developer."

The receptionist smiled and said, "Good morning, Mr. Newman. Welcome to TypTown. I'm Janice, and if there is anything I can do to help, just let me know. Please have a seat and I'll notify IS that you're here." As John sat down, Janice picked up the phone and told someone at the other end that John was waiting in the lobby.

Waiting for his IS contact to show up, John dreaded the usual long delay with nothing to do. But within two minutes after he had sat down, a man appeared from a hallway. "Hello, John?"

"Yes, I'm John Newman." John stood up and extended his hand.

The man grabbed it firmly and shook it. "I'm Bill Felder. I'll be your IS mentor during your orientation. We're sure glad to have you here at TypTown Samples. Before we start with the usual forms to fill out and all the introductions, let me buy you some coffee and a doughnut, OK?"

"Sure." The two men walked past a smiling, waving Janice and headed down the hall to the cafeteria.

After Bill paid for their food and drink, the two men sat down and began to chat. Bill appeared to be impressed when John told him why he had left HS to work for TypTown.

"Twin boys, huh? I can't think of a better place to raise kids than right here in Typical Town."

Bill was also surprised to learn that John had just become a second generation TypTown Samples employee. "We don't have very many people following in the family footsteps around here. I've only been here two years and, frankly, I've heard a lot of horror stories about the way TypTown used to run the show."

John appreciated having a mentor who would criticize his own company, realizing that Bill was not a company "yes man." But John was even more intrigued by the words "used to run."

As the two men ate and drank, Bill filled John in on some details John had failed to uncover while interviewing with TypTown Samples. "Just before I got here, old man Harris

11

finally retired and his daughter Donna took over the family business."

John remembered his father's complaints about TypTown and the "old man." Martin Gregory Harris was the founder of the company and one of the world's foremost experts on samples. It was Harris's driving vision that saw a tiny start-up company grow into the town's largest employer. He was constantly telling his employees, "If we don't produce the best damn samples in the world, the productivity of our sales reps will plummet. We have a serious burden to carry." In his mind, John pictured a sour-faced white-haired man straight out of a Dickens novel.

Bill said, "The bottom line is that Martin Gregory Harris was old fashioned and Donna isn't. You know, she graduated from Very Prestigious University. Donna has made sweeping changes in how TypTown operates."

"According to my father, anything would have been an improvement."

Bill smiled. "From what I've heard about how it used to be, that's probably true. But these changes would be good for almost any company."

A few minutes later they entered the IS Department, which wasn't too far from the main entrance. As they walked down the main aisle, John noticed three people huddled in a cube, talking intently. In John's experience, when that many people met in a developer's cube, somebody had a serious coding dilemma.

"If any of these people need help, I'll be glad to lend my expertise," John volunteered. "HS trained me quite well in Z."

"Thanks, John. I'll pass that on to some of our people. But I don't think those sample engineers want to hear about Z." Bill pointed to the next cubicle on the left. "This one is yours."

"Sample engineers?"

"Yup," said Bill as they sat down in John's new cube. Bill pointed across the aisle. "See the guy in the blue polo shirt? That's Tom Sparks. He's the only application developer in that group and he also knows Z pretty well. The other two people are from Sample Engineering."

"What are they doing in an IS Department? I've never heard of the users being on our turf before. At HS, we..."

"It's part of the changes that Donna Harris made. We used to be located in the basement, near the storage area. She moved us upstairs, right smack in the middle of the building."

"Why?"

"Because she wants to encourage our customers to come to see us. We never had any visitors in the basement and, to be honest, we kind of liked it that way. But she feels it's important that we be visible, not invisible. So here we are. She truly believes that IS is the heart of the company."

"Think of it this way, John," he continued. "We pump out data to every single part of the organization, figuratively and literally. Think where TypTown would be without us. We need to be in the center of things—again, literally and figuratively. Not that we had a choice about moving, but we couldn't argue with that logic."

"Is this setup working? It's really distracting to have users interrupting when you're trying to develop software."

"At first it was. But we're getting used to it. The customer interactions really help us understand the business and they're seeing that we're more responsive to their needs. Sure, the interruptions can be annoying at times. But sometimes they can also be extremely valuable."

"Let me give you an example," Bill continued. "I was working on the financial system a few months ago when one of our accountants came to see me about the project. It was a good thing she stopped by, because I was off track and didn't know it. If we had still been in the basement, I would have spent three weeks working on the software, going in the wrong direction, and not have known it until it was too late. Then it would have taken me four weeks to undo the mess I created for myself. It also meant that we would have been late with the project, and that certainly wouldn't have helped anybody. Now I don't mind interruptions anymore. Plus, because our customers now see what we're doing, we get more recognition and appreciation."

"And, John, notice that we don't refer to the other people around here as 'users.' They're customers and should be treated accordingly."

Different, Very Different

A moment later a woman knocked and entered John's cube. John immediately recognized her as Ana Hooper, the Director of IS. Ana and John had met when he had interviewed with TypTown.

After exchanging the usual pleasantries, John said to Ana, "Bill was explaining that you don't use the word 'users' here."

Ana nodded. "That's right. It's really important to have the right mindset. When you buy groceries or clothing or go to a restaurant, would you want to be called a 'user?' "

"Probably not," John said. "But I always treated my users - I mean my customers - with respect."

Ana smiled and said, "We know, John. One of the main reasons we hired you is for your people skills. Let me explain: when most computer people use the term 'users,' they think more about the systems than about the customers who are using them. While many in the computer industry call their department Information Technology or Information Systems, we chose Information Services. We chose not to be called IT because our focus is truly on providing service about information, not on managing technology or systems although that's a major part of what we do. When we think of customers, we think about the people who use the systems we create and maintain. We aren't necessarily hired to write beautiful code or play with the latest and allegedly greatest technology. Our goal is to give our customers solutions to their business issues. See the difference?"

John nodded and said, "I never thought of it that way," although he was still a bit confused. So far, the distinction didn't sound especially important to him.

Ana told John that she knew some of TypTown's ideas were new and different for John, but not to worry. She then looked at her watch and excused herself. "Got a meeting with Donna." She was gone as quickly as she had entered.

Bill stood up. "Maybe I didn't fully explain to you earlier that I'm your mentor, John. I'm here to help orient you to TypTown and to the IS Department in particular. We do things differently around here – better than most software shops, actually. Because of that, we found that new employees adjust more easily if they have someone to show them the ropes and answer their questions."

"We consider ourselves unique for a software shop. I don't mean that arrogantly. I just mean that our operating philosophy isn't typical. It differs quite a bit from what you experienced at HS. Don't worry, all the new people been able to make the adjustment."

"All?"

"Yes, John, every single one of them. One of the big reasons is that we're very careful about who we hire. As Ana mentioned, your people skills are crucial. Around here, we don't go for the super-techie. You know the type—the stereotypical developer who knows everything about coding except why he's doing it. We go for the whole package: people skills and technical aptitude.

"We can talk more about this later. Right now, you've got some paperwork to fill out or else HR is going to be all over me." Bill pointed to a folder that had been sitting on John's desk and excused himself so John could work on the inevitable forms.

As soon as Bill left, for some unknown reason, John thought about his friend Wes for a brief instant.

As he filled in names and numbers, John thought, "OK, so far, so good. The people sure seemed happy when I first met them at the interview but I figured it was to make a good impression on me. But maybe there really is something more to this place."

It took the rest of the morning to finish the paperwork because John was interrupted several times by his new coworkers, who dropped by to introduce themselves. As the new kid on the block, John appreciated their friendliness. He mentally compared the morning to his first few weeks at HS, where the attitude toward new people was "don't be seen or heard." He clearly liked TypTown's approach better.

At lunchtime, Bill dropped by John's cube with Tom Sparks, now done with his meeting, and made the introductions. Bill and Tom took him to Barretto's Pizzeria, which had been one of John's favorite hangouts during his high school years. "Humongous City never had a pizza place like this one," John told Bill and Tom.

The three men made small talk over a sausage and pepperoni pizza. Then Tom said something so unexpected that John almost choked: "It's only a matter of time before TypTown overtakes HS and becomes the country's leading supplier of samples."

"But HS is so big," John protested.

"Yes they are, John," Tom said. "And they make some pretty good samples, too. But they've become old and stodgy in their ways—kind of like TypTown when Donna's father ran the show. Since then we've taken giant leaps forward. We've always made good samples, but now we're doing things so much more efficiently."

"So how did TypTown take the giant leaps?" asked John.

"Donna Harris taking over for her father got us started. It's kinda surprising he turned the company over to her; their styles are so different. But it was that difference that began to change the culture and we needed that to happen," replied Tom.

Bill continued, "Donna had lots of knowledge and lots of new ideas but she didn't do it alone. She hired Earl Sandoval. He's an organization development consultant."

"Earl worked with us to help design and implement a lot of changes and it turned out we had many of the answers within us. Earl helped us realize that. He also understood that as our work processes changed, so did our jobs."

"What was really freaky," interrupted Tom, "was that he helped us see that the same thing happens to our customers when we implement a new system. A technology change also means a change to someone's job. There is a whole human element to our work that we never realized before."

"People would whine and complain about the most trivial stuff whenever we installed new software, regardless of whether it was a major or minor implementation. We thought they were just difficult users, pardon my use of that word. But Earl showed us it was really a reaction to a change in their job and I must admit I did some of the same things when our department changed."

"Thanks to Ana and Earl, the internal customer is much more connected to us and we work with whoever is affected at the beginning, not at the end like we did before. TypTown now has a Training Department to teach our customers the new systems, we involve the customers in the model office testing, we communicate with them better and more frequently and they are actively involved. It hasn't eliminated all the complaints but the number has been dramatically reduced."

"Earl showed us how to develop change management plans for affected people whenever there is new software that is going into production. And it was interesting to compare our initial reactions and behaviors to all the changes going on in our department to our customers. Earl helped us see that there were patterns between what we experienced and what our customers experienced," said Bill.

Toward the end of the day, Bill and John walked over to the Accounting Department, where Bill introduced John to some of the accountants. As John was shaking hands and exchanging greetings with these men and women, a man whom John already knew joined the crowd. He was Jim Grant, the head of Cost Accounting, who had been one of the people who had interviewed John at TypTown Samples.

"Good to see you again, John," Jim said. "Welcome to TypTown."

The introductions completed, most of the other men and women drifted back to their own work stations, but Jim stayed behind.

John said to him, "Jim, I have to ask you a question. I was afraid to ask this at the interview, but now that I'm a part of TypTown, let me ask it now. Why was I interviewed by both you and Ana? I can understand Ana doing it because of her position, but you're in Cost Accounting, not IS."

Jim smiled and nodded. "First of all, don't ever be afraid to ask a question around here, of me or anybody else. You can't learn by being quiet and you won't get beaten up for asking. Second, to answer your question, Ana and I conducted the cultural part of your second interview. You got a lot of technical questions when you first met with our people. By the time Ana and I met you, we were already serious about hiring you, and your technical knowledge was not an issue. But since you're going to support my people, I needed to see if you'd fit with the personalities in my department. Ana was doing the same thing for IS. If you're going to be working with my people - your customers - doesn't it make sense for me to spend a little time getting to know you?"

"It does seem logical," replied John.

"Logical!" Jim said loudly and with a laugh. "Just the word I'd expect a computer guy to use. See you tomorrow." And with that remark, the men parted ways.

Bill and John headed back to IS to finish out the day.

"Your training will start for real tomorrow," said Bill. "Some people take to it naturally; some suffer through it; but after some time, they all agree it is valuable. We can talk about it more tomorrow morning. I'll buy you another doughnut."

29

When John got home that night, Marilyn
anxiously asked about his first day at his new
job.

John's head was still spinning from
trying to absorb all he had been through. "It was
different, very different, from what I imagined
it would be. I don't profess to understand it all,
but something tells me this is going to be OK."

I'm An Accountant?

That evening, thanks in part to the short commute, John spent some quality time with Tony and Kirby before putting the boys to bed.

John was pretty tired himself. He realized it hadn't been TypTown that had caused him so much anxiety, but the anticipation and then the reality, of the new job.

John slept much better than the previous night and awoke at his usual time. In the morning John found himself looking forward to the day's events.

Once again John had a light breakfast, in part because he remembered Bill's promise of a doughnut.

"How long do you think that'll last?" his wife responded.

"I don't know," John replied, "but a free doughnut is something I never got at HS."

When John entered TypTown, Janice stopped him. John started to remind her that he was a new employee, but Janice interrupted him.

"I know who you are. You're John Newman, our new top-notch computer guru. I stopped you because Bill was out here so fast yesterday that we didn't have a chance to chat."

John was amazed at how Janice could talk to him while smiling and waving at everyone who entered the building. "This woman is waaay too friendly for Humongous City," he thought to himself.

A few minutes later, Bill appeared, and they headed to the cafeteria for the promised doughnut.

"What's the plan for today?" asked John.

"I'll turn you over to Jim," replied Bill, "He'll make sure you know the ins and outs of cost accounting."

John looked at Bill quizzically. "But I'm an application developer, not an accountant."

Bill chuckled and said, "Relax, relax. We know what you are."

"So why are you trying to change me? This isn't some sort of weird reassignment, is it?"

Bill saw John's face contort several times. "Relax, John. It's only for a few weeks so you can learn your customer's business from their point of view. Then we'll bring you back from the 'evil' of Cost Accounting into the 'light and goodness' that is IS."

"A few weeks!"

Bill smiled. "You'll spend a little time doing clerical work, getting to know your customers, and using the system that you'll soon be supporting. Trust me, it's only temporary, I promise. Now, are you ready to count beans?"

The two men got up and walked to Cost Accounting. They found Jim in his office looking over some reports. Jim's head lifted and he said, "Mornin', Bill. Mornin', future CPA."

"He's joking," laughed Bill to a not-so-amused John.

John stood there silently trying to figure out what to say or do next.

Bill told Jim, "I told John you'd teach him the ins and outs of cost accounting. He's all yours."

"That's debits and credits, not ins and outs, Bill." He turned to John. "Come on. Let's introduce you to the gang and get you started."

Within an hour, John found himself inside a Cost Accounting cube doing data entry work, interrupted only by the occasional delivery of an engineering form that reported cost changes on custom-made samples.

His first day on the job had gone so fast and so well. Now he couldn't believe how slow the second day was going.

In the afternoon, Bill and Ana dropped by to see how he was doing, but John didn't say much.

When John went home that night, Marilyn could tell he had had a bad day just by looking at him. Playing with the boys helped, but not much.

"Say something to your boss," said Marilyn. "Be assertive."

John agreed, but only halfway. He knew she was right but decided he'd be a good corporate soldier but only until he couldn't take it anymore.

As they began preparing the evening's meal, the doorbell rang.

Marilyn answered the door. When she opened it, Wes was standing on the other side. Marilyn invited Wes in and he immediately asked John how the new job was going before insisting the Newmans come to the Turners' home for dinner the following week.

John recapped the events of the past two days, knowing that he sounded unhappy.

Wes said, "Well, it's only day two. Day three could be totally different. And if not, think about CS. We're just starting a rewrite of our inventory system. It's all new development; it should be really interesting. As a matter of fact, my boss has spent the last few days talking to the inventory people to gather requirements for the work we're about to do. If something opens up, you'd be a great addition to the team."

Listening to Wes speak, John knew that he meant to be comforting. Yet all his words did was make John jealous.

The Big, Thick File

A few weeks of data entry and filing went by. John found the work easy but terribly tedious, and he was grateful for the occasional appearance of an engineering cost change form. He also appreciated the cheer-up calls he got from Wes. They were a pleasant distraction, but they also made John envious of Wes. After a month at his new job, John was just about ready to give Crusedome Systems a call.

One day Jim Grant dropped by to check up on John. "How's it going?" Jim inquired cheerily.

"Fine," lied John in return.

"Your analyses of those engineering cost changes are right on the money, John."

"Thanks."

"Get it? Right on the money? Ya know, *money*?"

"Well," thought John, "at least Jim thinks he's funny." John wasn't in a humorous mood these days.

"Seriously, John. Your analyses have been outstanding. Thanks for your diligence," said Jim, handing John a big, thick file. "Here. I'd like you to review this file when you have a chance. Let me know what you think of it." A moment later he was gone.

After Jim left, John just stared at the big, thick file. He wasn't an accountant and he didn't want to become one. Yes, he had learned a great deal about the Cost Accounting computer system and he had gotten to know his customers. But he found his current duties extremely dull—and now he dreaded having to analyze the contents of this big, thick file.

When John realized the file wasn't going to get any smaller merely by his wishing, he decided Marilyn was right—it was time to assert himself.

John marched into Ana's office.

"Hi, John. Come on in," Ana said, although John was already well into her office. "Jim tells me you're doing a great job in Cost Accounting."

"Thanks, but I'm not an accountant," John said quickly. "When do I get to do what I was hired for?"

"Soon. I promise."

"How soon? Jim just gave me this big, thick file to review. I don't mind the computer-related stuff, but this file is so thick, it can't possibly have anything to do with supporting the Cost Accounting computer system."

Ana smiled and said, "You'll be back in IS within a week. Now let me ask you: have you learned who your customers are? Are you thinking about their needs—putting yourself in their shoes?"

"Well, I've learned a little about the system. And the people seem nice."

"Right now, John, your job is to learn what works for them and why, what their constraints are and what you can do to make their jobs easier. And make no mistake about it: we hired you to make their jobs easier. We're a support department, not a profit center. Your salary ultimately comes out of their budget. You weren't hired to write code; you were hired to provide business solutions. Obviously, this will primarily be done through maintaining and enhancing the Cost Accounting system, but if you think of something else, by all means, tell us your suggestions. We're hungry for your input. And, John, don't worry about that file. Jim won't give you anything you can't handle."

"Oh, and one last thing, John. I appreciate your coming here to talk. It's your job to make Cost Accounting's job easier, and it's my job to make your job easier. You support Jim and his people and I'm here to support you."

Somewhat mollified, John thanked Ana for her time and returned to Cost Accounting.

He liked what she said, but he still had serious doubts. "Right words," he thought. "Now, let's see if she can back them up."

John stared at the big, thick file for what seemed like an eternity, then let out a heavy sigh, pulled it toward him, and opened it.

The first piece of paper was a printout of an old email discussing the correlation between productivity and the number of trips to the restroom.

John laughed as he realized that this was a joke email. He set it aside, thinking that Jim had put it in the file by mistake.

A few seconds later he realized how wrong he was. The entire file was filled with more joke emails, articles and cartoons.

He was laughing out loud when Jim and Ana dropped by half an hour later.

"You looked a little tense," said Jim. "I thought this would help."

John tried to thank him but was laughing too hard.

Ana said, "You have no idea how difficult it was to keep a straight face when you told me about the file Jim gave you. That file is legendary around here."

"Fifteen years of office humor," continued Jim. "I'm always adding to it, so if you come across something funny and it won't get me fired, bring it to me."

John's disposition lightened up considerably. Within the week he was back in IS, just like Ana had promised.

Who Owns The Software?

John's first assignment was a small maintenance project. It wasn't very challenging but, as Bill explained, this type of work was a good way to learn the existing system. John knew he'd be given this type of work until he developed the necessary understanding of TypTown's cost accounting system from a technical perspective.

Bill told him, "The process of how we operate is as important as your enhancements, both now and in the future. Review this IS Software Request Form and let me know when you are ready to see Wayne Orr."

"Why do we need to see Wayne?" asked John. John had met Wayne during his training and knew that he reported to Jim Grant in Cost Accounting. John noted that Wayne also was the one requesting that an on-line screen show the difference whenever a sample-related part changed price.

"PDSA, John. PDSA stands for Plan-Do-Study-Act. It's our customer service methodology. Earl Sandoval taught it to Ana and she passed it on to us.

"First, read through the request form and get an idea of what the customer wants and what it will take to make them—in this case, Wayne—happy. Once you know the background, you'll meet with Wayne to discuss his request. Make sure you're both on the same page. People frequently have different interpretations of the same words. The two of you will ensure that doesn't happen. That's the 'Plan' part."

Bill continued, "Then do a little work on Wayne's request. Don't spend a lot of time on it. Just prototype your results. Sometimes it's easier to use a piece of paper instead of the computer. If the request involves screen changes, like this one will, simply draw a box and write in what the change will look like. Or, if a report needs changing, write down the column headers so both of you can visualize the final outcome.

"Of course, in Z it's easy to whip up a quick and dirty version, if that's your preference - whatever works for you. This is the 'Do' part."

John said, "It sounds like you want me to do an experimental version of my response to his request, like a pilot study."

"Exactly right," replied Bill. "Now, the 'Study' part is where you meet with Wayne again. Show him your prototype so you can both study the results. If you're both in agreement that your pilot is good, you can start coding and testing. Then you get Wayne's final approval to go into Production - the 'Act' part. If he disagrees with your prototype - and in theory he shouldn't, because of the Plan step -

find out why, change your prototype, and loop through the process until he approves. Okay?"

"Sure. But customers don't always know what they want. You know, 'It's exactly what I asked for but not what I want.' "

Bill smiled and said, "You said 'customers,' not 'users,' John. We're beginning to have an effect on you."

John smiled, both pleased and a bit embarrassed.

Bill continued, "It's our customer's responsibility to know what they want. We don't play the 'It's exactly what I asked for but not what I want' game anymore. PDSA helps prevent that. So does ownership."

"Ownership?"

"Right, ownership. Who do you think owns the Cost Accounting system?"

"IS, of course," answered John. "IS designs, writes, and maintains the software, including the database tables, running the nightly batch jobs, handling the hardware, and all the other stuff."

"Not here at TypTown, John. That's another one of the differences between us and HS. Cost Accounting owns the Cost Accounting system: the software and the data. We in IS are heavily involved in it, but they own it."

"What difference does all this make?" asked John. "Isn't this splitting hairs?"

"No," said Bill, "It's more than symbolic. As the owners of the system, Jim, Wayne, and the rest of those folks have accountability. They're responsible for making sure the system works and functions to their liking. This includes making sure we have good specs to work with and that we are moving in the right direction. PDSA ensures that. Once something goes into production, that's it. As Ana told everyone at an all-company meeting, 'If we ever go back into a program for anything other than a change in business, it's much more than an IS screw-up.'"

"Wow. What was the reaction to that?"

"Donna Harris jumped to her feet and yelled, 'That's right! I love it!' More than anything else she did, that reaction told the whole company that the old way of doing business was dead."

Bill continued, "Ana has a good metaphor. Think about people you know that put on an addition to their home or had major remodeling work to their house. The general contractor brings in the construction workers, the plumber, the electrician, all those guys. They are all working on the plans agreed on by the homeowner and the general contractor. But the homeowner is involved, too. The homeowner has a say in the plans because it is his home and he's going to pay for the work. Now, let me ask you a question. Do you know a homeowner that's been in that situation?"

"Sure, I know a few families," replied John.

"Did those people just make the plans and write a check when the work was over?" asked Bill.

"No, now that I think about it, every one of them was always talking about how busy they were, running out to the store to pick out carpeting, wallpaper and cabinets. Heck, they even had to pick out the knobs on the new cabinets," said John.

"Exactly, John. The general contractor could have picked out all that stuff by himself and still remained within the homeowner's budget. But if the homeowner didn't like what the general contractor selected, the homeowner would have to replace those things at his extra cost or live with paying for something he didn't want. So to avoid those outcomes, he gets involved and takes ownership. It's his home, it's his responsibility," said Bill.

He continued, "And that is Ana's metaphor. Think of IS as the general contractor and, in your case, Cost Accounting as the homeowner. As the general contractor, you have your hands in all the software like the general contractor has his people inside the homeowner's house while they are doing the work. But the house still belongs to the homeowner and, for you, the software and the data still belong to Cost Accounting."

An Excellent DBA And A Lousy

Human Being

John did some preliminary investigating of Wayne's request while Bill attended a meeting in another department. The meeting ended at lunchtime, so Bill suggested that John join him and Tom for another pizza at Barretto's.

As the three men entered the pizzeria, they ran into a tall, scowling man who was leaving. "Hi, Tom. Hey, Bill. How's the new age voodoo going?" He didn't wait for a response, nor did he introduce himself to John, but quickly walked out to his car and drove off.

"Who and what was that all about?" asked John.

Bill and Tom both sighed heavily. Tom said, "That's P.T. Davis. He was a casualty of our changes."

"Actually," said Bill, "He was more like a casualty of himself not changing."

"True," said Tom. "P.T. was our database administrator. When Donna brought Ana on board and she started making changes, he refused to even try to adjust. No matter what, he liked the old way better. P.T. just kept on being his usual, surly self. Ana tried working with him, but it was futile. So she finally let him go."

Bill said to John, "He's an excellent DBA and a lousy human being. Nobody misses his temper tantrums, I can guarantee you."

"Yeah," said Tom. "Ana decided it was better to temporarily have a hole in the department than to keep a lingering cancer. We were hurting until we got a new DBA and got him up to speed but it was worth it. Jeez, you'd ask P.T. a question and he'd abuse you for the next 20 minutes."

Bill continued the dual storytelling as John looked at both men, his eyes shifting toward each speaker, as if he was watching a tennis match. "Ana gave the guy every chance to change. We found out later that she offered to give him a personal coach, send him to seminars on how to deal with people and all that stuff."

"P.T. was one of those people who can relate to computers but not to other people. The bottom line is that people aren't as logical as computers and he got angry whenever something doesn't go exactly like he thinks it should."

John asked, "He couldn't handle non-linear thinking?"

"That's a good way to phrase it," said Bill. "Firing him was the right thing to do. That was a rough day for Ana. She's not the kind of boss who likes to ax people, and P.T. wasn't exactly docile about it when she told him. But letting him go also sent a message to the rest of us. Think about it: Customer service, inside or outside IS, is important. It showed us she was serious about making the environment better at TypTown, and that she won't tolerate anyone on her staff being a jerk, no matter how talented they are."

"Is P.T. working for anyone now?" John asked.

Tom answered, "He's with KCI — Knowitt-Awle Consulting, Inc."

"I'm familiar with them," John said. "HS used their Humongous City branch. Or maybe I should say they used HS."

Bill snorted. "We used to be a cash cow for them, too. Ana wised up about them a year ago. They deserve P.T."

Tom said, "Now we only use consultants from CFC."

"Who are they?" asked John.

"Customer Focused Consulting," Tom said. "Their customer service attitude is compatible with ours. They look out for us; they don't try to create work just to stick around."

Bill said, "But we've kept them on because they keep creating value for us. They're so well integrated with us that we don't even talk about them as outsiders."

Suddenly, Tom started to laugh a little. "Remember the last time we saw that Knowitt-Awle Consulting sales rep? Geez, what was his name? I can picture him: short, stocky guy, always wore suspenders and thought he was smarter than everyone else."

"Dickey Bendorf!" replied Bill. "He thought he was pulling one over on Ana until she finally had enough. Here's this really good manager who is a really nice person and she got so fed up with his attitude and all the garbage he was feeding her, she stopped him in mid-sentence, announced that meeting was over and there would be no further communication with Dickey and his company. She got up and left, leaving Dickey standing there with his jaw on the ground and, at least for the time being, a little less arrogant. Knowing 'Bender' Bendorf, he probably went out for a three or four martini lunch, complaining about Ana the whole time and never realizing he shot himself in the foot."

"Got to be careful with consultants," observed Tom, opening a menu. "I don't know about the two of you, but I'm planning to stuff my face."

Living The New Way

That night after dinner, John, Marilyn, and the boys went over to see Ramsey. While Marilyn kept an eye on the kids, John told his father about the changes at TypTown.

"P-D-A-S?" asked Ramsey. "It doesn't exactly roll off the tongue, does it?"

John looked at his father and recalled what he himself has been recently experiencing. He realized that handling all kinds of new information at once was not a Newman family trait.

"PDSA, Dad. Plan-Do-Study-Act."

"Beats the hell out of waiting six months for you computer guys to start a project, then hear nothing for six more months, only to end up with a system that doesn't help. Man, the computer guys we had when I worked there drove everybody crazy with their inability to get anything done. They'd give us an estimate and disappear. Later, they would emerge with some goofy thing that didn't help us at all."

John decided it was time to give his wife, or really himself, a break and went to watch the boys. He was quite uncomfortable hearing the same complaints he had heard while at HS.

The next morning John went to see Wayne Orr in Cost Accounting. They spoke about his current assignment for a few minutes and Wayne gave John the information he needed. But as John got up to go, he astounded himself by saying, "When I was working over here, I learned that the percentage of any price change is important, but I noticed that it doesn't show up automatically on any screen. We should start adding it. We can easily show it right next to the price change itself."

"That would be great," Wayne said. "Show me what you have in mind."

"Sure. Let me just sit down at your computer."

John logged onto the system, pulled up information on a part, and made a screen print. He placed the screen print in front of Wayne and said, "The price change and the percentage change can go right here, right after the part description." John wrote sample data on the screen print to illustrate his point.

Wayne studied the page for a few seconds. "Super idea, John. Let's do it! If you like, I'll be happy to talk to Jim about bringing you back to us."

John laughed. "Right. My dream job."

Back in IS, John gave Bill an update.

"So what you're saying, John, is that you knew what your customer needed. Now you'll only be going into the software once instead of once now and again later on. So you worked with your customer, identified what had to be done, and then exceeded his expectations."

"Yep. Now can I have the rest of the month off?"

"Sure. And your Nobel Prize is waiting for you at Janice's desk."

John laughed. "Since we have to learn our customer's work and since they own the system and the data, shouldn't we make them do a little coding? It only seems fair."

Instead of laughing, Bill replied, "You sound like a volunteer."

John suddenly realized he had just said something he shouldn't have. He imagined himself turning into Homer Simpson and shouting "D'oh!"

"Just kidding, John. Geez, you look kind of pale."

The blood slowly returned to John's face as Bill explained, "You do have a point, though, and we do address it. In fact, we have a training seminar set up for a week from Tuesday."

"Training seminar? Volunteer? I'm confused."

"While Jim Grant and his bean-counters are your customers, you're also their customer. It's their responsibility to give you clear directions because they own the system and the data. That's why we train our customers in the basics of what we do. Ana puts the training on herself, but she's always looking for help, especially with the departmental specifics."

"Huh?"

"Ana goes over the basic stuff: what are records and fields, what a relational database is, an overview of object-oriented programming, the Agile development process, how everything works, what software can and cannot do, how to write a work request, that sort of thing. Then she likes the experts in each area to reinforce those concepts and teach the departments about their own systems, including the strengths and weaknesses and to answer questions. And if you think accountants ask a lot of questions, you should see Tom after he gets done with the sample engineers."

"How often are these sessions held? There must be a lot of them."

"Well, when Ana first started these things, it seemed like we were doing them all the time because we had so many people to train, but now it's on an as-needed basis. It's actually part of our standard new employee orientation. Because you're an ISer, we skipped it for you — we figured you know that stuff."

"I hated being an accountant. Now we have the home court advantage."

Bill said, "A lot of people didn't like this training. We had to drag them in, kicking and screaming. But about six months after we started these training courses and got accustomed to PDSA, the whole company noticed that we were getting things done better and faster and a lot less stressfully, too."

"The way I see it, PDSA and all this training on both sides really helps people communicate better. Like Ana told me earlier about putting yourself in your customer's shoes, the rest of TypTown is making an effort to step into IS' shoes," John said.

That night, John and his family hosted the Turners for dinner, returning the hospitality they had received earlier. When the doorbell rang, John opened it to see that all the Turners were all present except for one. After saying hello and herding her kids inside, a harried Jayne added, "I'm sorry, John, but Wes is still at the office. He'll try to join us as soon as possible. Things have been really hard with Wes's hours. Recently he's been putting in all kinds of overtime. It's been crazy."

John finally got a word in, "I can see. Well, come in and relax." Jayne took a deep breath, laughed a little and gave hugs to John and Marilyn, as the Turners entered the Newmans' home.

Wes finally arrived just as they were finishing dessert, Marilyn's renowned cake. He apologized, sat down, and gratefully began eating the food they had saved for him.

After a few minutes, the conversation turned to the training seminar TypTown Samples' IS Department conducts for its internal customers. Wes was amused at the idea. "John, that's giving too much information to people who don't have a clue as to what they want. The reason I've been putting in so much overtime lately is that my team was working on what the users wrote down in their software requests. Then, we wanted to show them the results of our coding. At first, they were too busy for us so we proceeded as best we could.

When they finally graced us with their presence, all we heard was 'Change this' and 'Change that.' I'm looking at them like, 'Where the hell did that come from?' My boss spoke to the users, wrote down their requirements and then - after we all worked hard on making them happy - they come back and tell us that we didn't understand what they wanted. And it was right there in black and white."

John let his friend vent his frustrations, remembering that Wes had allowed him to do the same for him when he had first started working in Cost Accounting. Then, at what John thought was an appropriate time, he told Wes about PDSA. He quickly realized that he had made a mistake.

"That sounds good, John," Wes said, "but we don't have time to try-new fangled things. We have real work to do."

John then tried to explain TypTown's theory of ownership to Wes, but Wes quickly interrupted him. "If our inventory people owned our system, they'd probably lose it, along with the other stuff in the warehouse they can't keep track of." Everyone could sense the anger behind that joke.

Later that evening, as the Newmans cleaned up after dinner, Marilyn said, "Wes looked awful tonight. I'm so glad you're not working the overtime you used to at HS. You're more relaxed and you seem much happier."

"It's good not to be fried by the end of the day," agreed John. "So this is what it is like to have a life!"

"I like the new you," said Marilyn. "And so do Tony and Kirby."

Plan For Success

Marilyn and the boys quickly adjusted to life in Typical Town. Even though he had felt he had sacrificed his position at HS for his sons, John had to admit he was enjoying his new job a lot more than the old one.

As John told his father more about the "new" TypTown, Ramsey couldn't believe some of it, especially when his son raved about what a great place it was to work. "HS must have been a really brutal place for you to like TypTown Samples," Ramsey said, shaking his head in disbelief.

"Actually, from what I've heard from my friends in the industry, it's a stereotypical IS environment. The difference is that TypTown aligns IS with the rest of the organization instead of viewing it as a necessary evil."

John was learning the Cost Accounting system quite quickly. Jim Grant even sent an email to Ana, complimenting John on his efforts. Ana passed it along to John along with her own congratulations.

On his way to the cafeteria for lunch one day, John couldn't help but notice that Bill was in an unusually good mood.

"Why the happy face? Did you win the lottery last night?"

"If I had done that, John, I'd be having an authentic Italian lunch - in Rome. But you're right, I'm happy. I was just made a team leader."

"Oh, yeah? Great! Congratulations!"

"Thanks. I'm going to head up the BAGEL re-write and the conversion from the mainframe to a web-based system."

"BAGEL?"

"It's our general ledger system. It's such a dog it was nicknamed BAGEL, for <u>B</u>and-<u>A</u>ided <u>GE</u>neral <u>L</u>edger. We put lots of Band-aids and work-arounds on that system over the years. I'll bet your father knows the guys who wrote it. It's been around a long time and the upgrade will be a quantum leap forward."

"Ana called me into her office this morning," Bill continued. "She said I'll be leading a team of five people when the project starts. It'll be announced soon."

"When do you start being the big cheese?" asked John.

"I'll start in a couple of months. First, I need to transition my work and take some leadership courses."

"Leadership courses? You don't need that stuff - you already know how to lead. You're a natural."

"Thanks for the compliment, but they want me to go anyway. Ana says it is part of the Plan for Success program."

John frowned. "Never heard of it. Does that mean I'm viewed as unsuccessful?"

"No, no, no, it's nothing like that. It's for the new leaders - to make sure we understand what our new jobs are all about. You know, there's a lot more to leading a team than most people realize. TypTown recognizes that and is quite proactive about it."

As they reached the cafeteria, they saw Ana coming out, carrying a cup of coffee. "Hi, Ana," Bill said. "I was just starting to tell John about the Plan for Success program."

"Oh, yes," said Ana. "That is one of Earl Sandoval's innovations."

"So what's Bill going to learn?" John asked Ana.

Ana took a sip of her coffee. "All about being a leader. There's a lot more to it than people think. John, let me ask you a question: What was IS leadership like at HS?"

John frowned again. "My manager knew our system inside-out. But it seemed like it was a big secret. We had to drag information out of him and, even then, we'd only get what we needed in bits and pieces."

"Let me tell you a little management secret," Ana said. "Good leadership breeds good leadership. Bad leadership breeds bad leadership. We want to make sure we have good leadership here. Nothing wrecks a company faster than a bad leader, and the computer industry has had more than its fair share of them. That isn't going to happen here anymore." She took another sip of coffee.

"That's why we started the Plan for Success program. Bill's going to learn about project management, communications, team dynamics, change management, corporate culture, and a whole lot more. We're going to give him all the tools he needs to be a success, from both a people and a project point of view, before he officially takes a leadership role."

"A lot of companies don't provide technical career paths for their people like we do, so when they need a team leader, they go to the person that knows the system the best. He's the most valuable one in the group, so he gets promoted. The problem is that he might not want or might not be prepared for his new role. Usually he doesn't have a choice, because it's the only way to get ahead in his company. He isn't necessarily a bad person. Plus, unlike, say, marketing, IS has a lot of introverted people in it. They can deal with a computer just fine. And there's nothing wrong with being introverted. But what happens when you force an introvert to give up what he was doing so well and put him in charge of people? Suddenly he needs to use skills that he doesn't have. Often, he doesn't even have the desire to use them. Everyone, including the manager, loses. No one likes working for him and he doesn't enjoy his job anymore but he's trapped in it because going back to what he enjoys is seen as a demotion."

"Wow...that's really interesting," said John, thinking about how much sense that made. "I guess my old boss wasn't a bad guy after all. He just couldn't communicate."

"Yes, that very well could be," Bill interjected. "Sadly, that situation happens far too often and nobody ever comes out it feeling good."

With that comment, Ana returned to work and John and Bill got their lunch.

That afternoon, when he needed a quick break, John called Wes and invited him to go fishing with him and Ramsey the following weekend. Wes jumped at the chance. "If that doesn't relax me, nothing will. Tell those fish that they'll soon be feeling the stress I'm under now." In the next breath, Wes launched into another tale of miscommunication between the software people and the inventory people on his project, resulting in yet another delay and more overtime. John offered all the empathy he could.

"Wes, when I first started working with the people over here, I thought the team leaders were surprisingly good. Then I found out the TypTown made them that way. They have a training program that deals with project management, team dynamics and a bunch of other hard skill and soft skill stuff. And here's the amazing thing: the team leaders go through this training *before* they start leading people. We don't throw our team leaders to the wolves like they did at HS. TypTown sets these people up to succeed."

"John, that's so simple, it's clever. It sure doesn't operate like that around here. My boss was happy about one of the other developers leaving the company last week. I heard she was in the boss' office a month or so ago, upset about who knows what, and she started crying. He's, like, 'get the hell out of here and start writing code.' He was happy about the woman leaving but she was a good developer and now the rest of us have to pick up the slack. Speaking of which…"

"I understand," said John, "see you later." As he hung up, his only thought was, "That sounded just like me when I was at HS."

Avoiding The Double Cost

A few days later, John received an e-mail from Tom Sparks. The message invited John to his project's kick-off meeting, some sort of CAD-CAM thing that John didn't understand. "That's odd," thought John, "I work with bean counters, not the Pocket Protector Brigade."

John dropped by Tom's cube later that day to confirm that John's invitation was not a mistake.

"No mistake," Tom said. "You're invited. Hope you can make it. And get there early before all the best refreshments are gone. Those sample engineers have lightning-fast reflexes when it comes to food."

"But why me, Tom? I'm not part of this project, and I already have a full plate with Jim Grant and his people."

"Well," Tom said, "Bill asked me to have you sit in on this meeting. It is IS's first new big project since you started here at TypTown and the first available kick-off meeting. He wants you to observe how we do things. Come, watch, and eat. After the meeting, if you like, you can give Bill a hard time for pressuring me to demonstrate a kick-off meeting to you."

On the day of the meeting, John arrived in the conference room a few minutes before the scheduled start time. John scanned the room and noticed almost every sample engineer already had a beverage in one hand and a plate of food in the other and remembered Tom's comment about how those engineers grabbed food so quickly. As he looked around, John saw a few people in the room that he knew, mostly coworkers of Tom. But he also recognized Karl Katzman, the head of the operations and hardware people. John couldn't understand why

Karl was in this meeting any more than he understood his own presence. The remaining people were all from Sample Engineering, including its vice president, George Walker. John smirked when he saw several pocket protectors.

Tom started the meeting exactly on time. He made a few opening remarks, then went around the room, introducing each person by name, position, and expected role on the project. When Tom introduced John and explained his presence as an observer, the new application developer heard a few friendly, welcoming comments from those in attendance.

Tom's introduction of Karl explained his presence to all. "This is Karl Katzman, manager of Computer Operations and Networking. He's been at TypTown for ten years and started as an operator and worked his way up. Karl is also the clean-up hitter on our championship softball team." This comment brought a round of friendly applause and a couple of whistles from those gathered. "Karl is here today because we anticipate the project will have heavy client server usage. This impacts Karl and his group and we want him to be prepared to assist with our networking and batch updates requirements. Karl?"

Karl nodded. "Our group's motto is 'The more the lead time, the better.' I appreciate being invited to this meeting. Remember, if I have everything dumped on me at the last minute, I'll need to put in some overtime…and I don't want to miss any ball games."

After completing the introductions, Tom spoke about the purpose of the project, how it would benefit TypTown and why senior management was sponsoring it. Then he began explaining the administrative and logistical aspects of the project. Tom said that he and his Sample Engineering counterpart wrote the project charter and received senior management approval. George Walker interrupted to tell the group that Tom and his counterpart did an excellent job and it was easy for the leadership team to give its approval. "We'll also come up with a cool acronym for the project," added a pleased Tom.

As Tom explained each administrative detail, John found himself growing increasingly impressed. The project charter showed clearly defined roles, responsibilities, deliverables, descriptions, costs, change management plans, what needed to be included in the monthly status reports, and the purpose of the weekly team meetings (including who would facilitate them and who would take minutes). But what most impressed John was how the project charter was going to track and prioritize requirements and how a defined procedure would be used for approving changes, thus avoiding the always-present opportunity for scope creep.

When the meeting adjourned, George Walker approached John. "Aren't you Ramsey Newman's boy? Same last name, some family resemblance?"

After John pleaded guilty, George asked about how Ramsey was doing. "He put in a lot of good years for us," he said. "You make sure to tell him he's still appreciated around here."

"He'll be happy to hear those compliments, sir," said John, suddenly feeling about five years old.

"You know, I really didn't handle people well in the old days," said George. "I thought it was my job to crack the whip on everybody, whether they reported to me or not. I don't know how your dad put up with me."

John said simply, "Uh, he's a patient man, sir."

"I've learned a lot these last couple of years. When Martin Gregory Harris handed the company over to his daughter, I thought we would be out of business in a matter of months. But she persisted and she turned out to be right. One of the best things Donna did was bring in Ana Hooper. She's really kicked some butt in your department. You should have seen it a couple of years ago. In the old days, whenever we'd ask IS to do a project, it was always late and we never got what we wanted. Things got even worse when PCs took over the world, if you can believe it. IS was what I called a 'double cost.' First we'd pay for the IS screw-ups, then people outside your department had to spend extra time trying to straighten things out everywhere else. So we'd either buy our own software package or contract with a consulting firm to bring in some hired hands in to do the work we needed. That was the extra cost. Today it's different. Now we finally know how to communicate. We know what you guys can do and you know what our needs are. It didn't happen overnight, but IS is now an investment instead of a double cost."

"If you'll excuse me," finished George, "I have a leadership development coaching session with Earl Sandoval starting in a couple of minutes and I don't want to be late for it. But I'm glad to have met you." He shook John's hand and walked away.

"You've got to be kidding!" Ramsey said several days later, packing his gear for the fishing trip with John and Wes. "Are you sure it was the same George Walker?"

"Dad, I swear it's true. George Walker had nice things to say about you. And then he talked about how he's changed."

The phone rang. John put down his tackle box and grabbed it.

Wes was calling. "You wouldn't believe what we discovered late last night. We thought the inventory people wanted daily e-mail updates on price changes, and it turns out they wanted price updates in another form entirely. So, guess what? We're going back to the office for yet another long weekend. One of the guys joked, 'now that it's Friday, there are only two more days to work this week.' If they would have told us what they wanted when we asked them six weeks ago, all this could have been avoided. What a waste of time and effort. Everyone here is frustrated."

"And we're really in a time crunch because the end of the quarter is coming up fast and that's when the boss promised the users we'd have something ready for them – like we ever had a snowball's chance in hell of accomplishing that goal. I'm really sorry; I can't go fishing with you and your dad. And when – or should I say 'if' – I get home, I need to spend some time with Jayne and the kids. This project has been hard on her, too, but, hey, what can you do? I'm sorry, John. Catch a walleye and drink a lot of beer for me, okay?"

Ramsey was quiet as he watched John talk to Wes on the phone. Finally, as he finished packing, Ramsey said, "I want to hear more about what's going on at TypTown," his bewilderment apparent in his voice.

John, to his surprise, spoke about his adjustment to TypTown all the way up and onto the lake. He almost regretted telling his father what George Walker had said because Ramsey spent a good part of the fishing expedition talking about how everybody felt about George. The word "hated" was used repeatedly.

"Seemed like a good guy to me. He claims to have changed, Dad."

"I'll believe it when I see it," snorted Ramsey, "but I would rather stay away from him and not bother to find out for myself. I'm retired; I don't work for the company anymore.

Now let's change the topic and concentrate on what we came here to do."

And with that statement, the Newman men turned their focus to fishing. The fish had other ideas that day and the two fishermen, much to their chagrin, returned home empty-handed.

Welcome To The World Of ECOs

Day by day, John became more adjusted to living in Typical Town and to his job at TypTown. His fishing trips with his father gradually became ice-fishing trips, and just as gradually returned to fishing again. Wes was frequently invited but unable to join in most of the time.

One day, John received a request from Wayne Orr, who wanted to begin seeing monthly reports on sample parts with a 20% variance from the previous month. Later that afternoon, John walked over to see Wayne so they could plan the report.

The cost accountant was clearly exasperated when John entered his cube. "I'm going over these goofy engineering change orders," complained Wayne. "Why is it so hard to understand what the sample engineers are trying to say? Can't somebody teach them English?"

"Can I see one?" asked John.

Wayne handed over an engineering change order, or ECO, for short.

John looked over the sheet of paper. "What the heck is this?"

"Whenever the sample engineers switch parts or assemblies or rework them, we get these forms so we can track the cost differentials. They used to have engineering cost change forms, but in an effort to simplify matters — I don't know for who — that was eliminated. Now we're supposed to read and understand what a bunch of techno-geeks are trying to tell us. Uh, no offense, John."

"None taken. I just came by to talk about your request for a sample part cost variance report."

"I gotta tell you, John. Those engineers are going to cost us some big bucks one day.

Last month, I got this ECO saying a part number was changed to another part number that cost $56 more. With the number of total samples affected by the change, it had a $250,000 impact—and I was ready to report it all as a cost. At one point, I did all the work for my general ledger entry and had it double-checked and signed off by Jim Grant. But I just couldn't bring myself to put it into BAGEL. It kept bugging me. Why replace a part with one that costs so much more? Didn't make sense. I finally called the sample engineer and he told me it's a three dollar change for the total impact."

John was sure he hadn't heard Wayne correctly. "$250,000 versus three bucks?"

"Yep, that's what he said. I'm trying to figure out what planet he's from. I go down to see him with the ECO in hand, along with data on the part numbers. He looks at the ECO and still claims it's a minor change."

"That can't be. What finally happened?"

"We got lucky. Another sample engineer overheard us and came by. He was able to translate the ECO between engineer-speak and real people. The first guy wrote 'replaced part number 12754 with 144392.' It turns out that Sample Engineering physically changed part number 12754 into part number 144392 by adding a few wires to the assembly. I'm reading 'replaced' to mean 'removed and replaced with something from inventory;' he's thinking about adding wires. It turned out to be less than a four-dollar impact. But I could have written off $250,000 and nobody would have ever known there was an error." Wayne sighed. "I don't mean to whine to you, John; it isn't your fault. It just ticks me off, that's all. It was a close call."

"I can see why. Is now a good time to talk about your cost variance report request?"

"Yes," said Wayne. "Let's switch gears. It'll calm me down."

For the next several minutes, the two men talked about what needed to be done. The PDSA effort was getting easier and easier for John, especially when he was working with a knowledgeable customer like Wayne. John was especially impressed when Wayne suggested that John use the Inventory Received data to list the last five parts-received totals. Wayne's suggestion meant the report would show if volume purchasing or some other purchasing trend impacted the cost of a part.

After their discussion ended, John had a clear view of what he needed to do and Wayne had clear expectations. John started to leave, but a thought stopped him. He turned around and asked Wayne if he could make a copy of an ECO. Wayne offered to give them all to John.

"I just need to copy one," said John. "I'd like to play around with it. This intrigues me."

Helping The Customer Succeed

John looked over the ECO form. It was pretty generic. The instructions merely called for a technical description of the change, which sample lot was affected, a large box where the sample engineer documented the change and signatures from the sample engineer and his manager. Directions at the bottom stated that ECOs should be copied and sent to Purchasing and Cost Accounting.

John could see why Wayne hated dealing with ECOs. The one he had copied contained a drawing that looked like it came straight out of a blueprint. To the right of this drawing was some unintelligible scribble that he presumed described the drawing. Already John could see that some kind of change would need to be made.

A few days later, John was ready with the cost variance report. This time, Wayne came to John's cube to discuss it. "I wanted to get away from my desk. Those ECOs are piling up. I hate those things."

"Are they making a lot of changes over in Sample Engineering?" asked John.

"No, the damn things are piling up because it takes me a long time to determine the cost impact and that puts me behind in my other work. It's a little like having to deal with you computer guys before all of the changes were made around here."

"Well, I've got something that should make you happy," said John as he handed his cost variance report work over to Wayne.

The two discussed what John had done. Wayne liked what he saw, offering only a couple of minor modifications.

As Wayne left to return to Cost Accounting, John thought about what Wayne had said about the old days of dealing with IS. "It's another communication issue. The sample engineers are writing technical documents in geek language, which is then being read by non-technical people who don't understand it."

John stared at his copy of an ECO with his new insight in mind. Next, he quickly grabbed some paper and a ruler out of his desk and began drawing. On the left side, he drew a series of boxes for the type of change being made to the sample. Inside each box he placed smaller check-off boxes, labeled "Rework Part From," "Rework Part To," "Add Part," and "Delete Part."

On the right side of the form, John drew corresponding boxes in which the sample engineers could write down the affected part numbers. He wrote instructions stating that an ECO describing reworked parts must use both the From and To boxes before being accepted.

Below this series of boxes, John drew a large box for a technical description, followed by lines for signatures and routing instructions.

In less than 90 minutes, he had redesigned the ECO.

Excited, he went over to see Wayne. Wayne took one glance at John's handiwork and instantly recognized its value. "Let's go see Jim," he said.

The cost accountant and the application developer worked through the maze of cubes to Jim Grant's office. Wayne didn't even give Jim the chance to say hello before showing him John's new form.

"Will this help?" Jim asked as he looked over the hand-drawn page.

"Absolutely," said John. "Right now sample engineers are communicating technical changes to people who don't care why something is being done; they only want to know the impact of the change. The form I've created allows the sample engineers to easily and clearly state the impact to others without having to bog them down with details."

Wayne added, "Yes, we don't care why a change is being made; we only care about its cost impact. And I know Maria Soto in Purchasing also has trouble with the ECOs. Sometimes she doesn't buy the necessary supplies on time because she can't understand what she is supposed to do. John's form takes all the guesswork out. It will be more accurate and it'll help people like Maria and I do our work faster."

"Excellent!" said Jim. "I'll give George Walker a call and ask about changing his form. John, are you sure you don't want to come back here permanently? I'll find you a real nice cube."

"Oh, look at the time," John said. "I've left a cake in the oven and the water running and I'm running terribly late for something or other."

Celebration Time

A few months later, at the quarterly all-IS staff meeting, Bill gave the group an update on the re-writing of BAGEL. He concluded by saying, "There's one last task we need to complete at this stage. We need a new acronym to replace BAGEL, because the system won't be a Band-aid much longer. Anyone who has a suggestion, please bring it to me."

Bill suddenly smiled and looked straight at John. "And now let me turn the meeting over to our fearless leader, Ana Hooper."

John looked around the room. Wayne Orr, Maria Soto, Jim Grant, and George Walker were all standing near the conference room door. He couldn't figure out why they were there and became more bewildered when the door opened and Donna Harris joined that group.

They all walked to the front as Ana took control of the meeting. "Now comes the cool part of my job," she said. "We want to present John Newman with a plaque and a bonus for his outstanding problem solving and contributions to TypTown. Come up here, John."

The rest of the department applauded as a surprised John walked up to accept his unexpected reward.

Jim explained to the group what John had done with re-designing the ECO form and how much it had helped. "Wayne and Maria's work is being done faster, easier and more accurately," he said.

George added, "Without any impact on my people in the process."

Donna said, "Note that John created a win-win situation for all concerned. And he didn't need to write a single line of code to do it. He used his ingenuity and intelligence to develop a business solution. Not only that, he did all this without anyone asking him; he took the initiative. That's why we hired him. That's why we hired all you good people."

After the meeting adjourned, Ana privately told John his salary was increasing, as part of his reward.

John called Marilyn with the good news and suggested that the Newman's and their friends the Turners go out for dinner to celebrate. But when the two families gathered at the restaurant, there was one person missing. Wes was working late again.

Another New Beginning

Time passed because, well, that's what time does. Now, John had become a mentor at TypTown Samples himself.

One morning, he was chatting in his cube with Bill and Tom, waiting for Janice to call him from the lobby. Bill was giving John some good-natured ribbing. "Remember, it's your responsibility to buy the new guy a doughnut. I'm going to casually drop by, too, so you can finally buy one for me."

Janice bailed out John by calling to say that the new employee was waiting for him in the lobby.

As he took the short walk down the hall, John wondered how big Jim Grant's joke file was by now. He smiled as he anticipated the day Jim would hand it over to TypTown's newest application developer.

John stepped into the lobby and greeted the man. "Hello. It's really good to see you here. Welcome to TypTown Samples."

"Thanks, John," replied Wes, smiling. "I'm excited to be here."

Key Alignment Points

1. To properly align IS, the whole organization needs to change. The organization's reward systems must fit the desired outcomes.

2. IS deals with customers, not users, and these people should be treated accordingly.

3. It is IS' role to generate business solutions. Writing code or using technology is not as important as helping customers succeed.

4. Internal customers own the software systems and have the accountability that goes along with that ownership.

5. PDSA enhances communication and reduces rework.

6. Train IS leaders on the people skills they need to be successful. Be proactive with this training whenever possible.

7. Acknowledge past mistakes; they are a great source of learning.

8. Involve internal customers in the hiring process to ensure that candidates fit the organization's culture.

9. Orienting new employees to the company and, in particular, to their internal customers is critical.

10. Bringing consultants into the organization requires great care and scrutiny. Make sure the consultant's skills and values fit the organization's needs and culture.

11. Poor communication and poor planning create stress on an organization and its employees and will inevitably lead to rework and turnover.

A Final Note

Think about how both the company, Typtown, and the individual contributor, John, had to culturally change. The new attitude Donna Harris brought to the company was reflected consistently in actions, both large and small including the hiring of like-minded leaders like Ana Hooper and providing coaching to help George Walker adjust to the new leadership style.

As the culture changed for John, he was surrounded by help. He had a mentor and support from his colleagues and managers as he went through his adjustment. Note that Typtown rewarded John for demonstrating the right behaviors and values.

- What actions are you taking to understand your colleagues on the other side of the business – IS continuum?

- What actions are you taking to have your colleagues on the other side of the continuum understand you?

- Who are the colleagues you can partner with to implement change, even if it is a small one?

- What are the barriers to alignment and what can you do to reduce or remove them?

Acknowledgments

Thank you to Lawrence Sahulka for designing the cover and Andrea Stowe for the illustrations.

Thank you to the friends and colleagues who reviewed and critiqued the manuscript and provided support for this project, especially Pat Morris and Paul Miller.

To Dr. Glenda H. Eoyang, who was kind enough to write the foreword.

And mostly to you, the reader, in the hopes that the ideas in this book helps your company achieve its desired goals.

About the Author

Varied roles in both software and business along with a proven ability to improve processes and implement change has given Al Strauss a multilayered view of how business and software can successfully connect.

For his coding, testing, business analysis, change management and communication work, Al has worked with General Motors, Target, Cargill, Medtronic, General Dynamics C4 Systems and others.

Al holds a Bachelor of Science in Business Administration from Minnesota State University, Mankato and a Master of Arts in Human Resource Development with a concentration in Organization Development from the University of St. Thomas.

In his spare time, Al listens to a variety of music (and is a big fan of Booker T and the MGs), plays hockey, watches movies and enjoys learning. He resides in Bloomington, Minnesota.

Comments and feedback are always welcome. Al can be contacted at: al@alstrauss.com.